dùn Chàrlabhaigh

and the Hebridean Iron Age

Ian Armit &

This guidebook and the new Visitor Centre at Dùn Chàrlabhaigh were conceived, organised and brought to completion by *Urras nan Tursachan and An t-Seana Bheinn* with the enthusiastic support of the community of Doune Carloway and of *Carloway Historical Society.* To these bodies, and to our many new friends among their ranks, the authors offer their thanks.

Historic Scotland provided time for writing and funding for new illustrations. John Hope brought us up to date on his ideas about broch architecture. Alan Braby drew the new illustrations, and redrew them as our ideas changed. James Smith supplied splendid photographs to replace most of our amateur efforts.

Permission to reproduce existing images was generously given by *Historical Scotland,* the *Royal commission on the Ancient and Historical Monuments of Scotland , Comhairle nan Eilean Siar (Museum nan Eilean), Edinburgh University,* Chris Burgess and Alan Braby. Copyright remains with these and with the authors.

The publishers acknowledge financial assistance towards this publication from the following: *Historic Scotland, Western Isles Enterprises, Western Isles Council, Western Isles, Skye and Lochalsh LEADER.*

First published in Scotland in 1998 by Urras nan Tursachan Ltd.
© 1998 Urras nan Tursachan
© Ian Armit and Noel Fojut

Front cover photograph: James Smith.
Artifact photographs: John MacLean Photography.
Sketch of the Dùn Chàrlabhaigh Interpretive Centre by Michael Leybourne.

Design and typesetting by Acair Ltd., Stornoway, Isle of Lewis
Printed by J Thomson Colour Printers, Glasgow.

ISBN 0 9532906 0 3

Contents

FOREWARD

We who live in the west of the Island of
Lewis are singularly blessed with an
extraordinary rich and diverse
archaeology, which has captivated the
interest of ourselves and our visitors for
many years.

Dùn Chàrlabhaigh – An Dùn Mòr –
arguably the most prominent legacy
which our ancestors bequeathed to us –
was built by our forebears at the dawn of
the Christian era. It is a tribute to their
skill that this fine drystone building –
known to archaeology and the wider
world as a broch, still stands today. It is
salutary to consider that when Dùn
Chàrlabhaigh was built the main part of
the Standing Stones of Calanais just a
few miles down the road was already
three thousand years old – a thousand
years older than Dùn Chàrlabhaigh is
today!

Both of these world famous monuments
to the past are in the care of
Historic Scotland, who are joined with
our community and other public bodies
in the partnership of *Urras nan Tursachan*,
the Trust responsible for building and

managing the new Visitor's Centres at
Calanais and Dùn Chàrlabhaigh. The
authors of this most excellent new book,
both members of *Historic Scotland's*
professional staff, are quite simply the
experts in their field. They are to be
congratulated on their work which brings
the benefit of their extensive knowledge
to a wide and grateful audience.

Simon Fraser
Calanais

Dun Carloway is an English version of Dùn Chàrlabhaigh
and has been commonly used in this form for many years.

Dùn Chàrlabhaigh/Dun Carloway in History and Legend

Early accounts

Until well into the 19th century, most antiquities were regarded simply as part of the landscape. Apart from occasional references to castles, churches and standing stones, few early writers on the Western Isles describe them: Dean Munro (1549), for example, omits any mention of the broch at Carloway, as does Martin Martin (1695). Thomas Pennant and his corespondent did not reach Lewis, nor did James Boswell and Dr Samuel Johnson. It is not until 1797 that the broch at Carloway appears in print, in the first Statistical Account, where it is laconically described by the local minister as 'perhaps the most entire of any of the kind in Scotland'. At this date brochs were thought to be either watch-towers against Viking raids or else to have been built by the Vikings (or 'Danes') themselves.

Antiquarianism arrives

All this was to change in the later 19th century, as antiquarian interest grew in earnest. Brochs were an early focus of study; it was soon demonstrated that they pre-dated the Vikings by several centuries, and belonged to the Iron Age, at first defined roughly as approximating to the period when the Romans occupied southern Britain. It was Captain Thomas who made the first reliable records of Western Isles brochs. His account, not published until 1890, described Dun Carloway as it was 30 years earlier and includes the first known drawing, showing the structure much as it looks today. It was on the basis of Thomas's description and enthusiastic reports from the first Inspector of Ancient Monuments that Dun Carloway was taken into State care in 1887.

DUN CARLOWAY FROM THE WEST

DUN CARLOWAY FROM THE EAST

Late 19th century drawing of Dun Carloway – the upper wall appears more complete than nowadays.

Systematic recording

It was to be another generation before a detailed record of the monument was made by the *Royal Commission on the Ancient and Historical Monuments of Scotland* in 1921. By this time the upper part of the outer wall had already been repaired and the interior cleared of loose rubble. This early records show that the left hand chamber in the wall-base was unrecognisable, being choked with fallen masonry, and that the chamber opposite the entrance was also almost as badly collapsed.

Early 20th century photograph of Dun Carloway, showing the blackhouses in use.

Completing the picture

It was not until 1971 that this last part of the broch was excavated, the shape of this chamber established and the wall consolidated. It was found that the cell had been used either for making pottery vessels or as a rubbish tip for large amounts of broken pot fragments and other material. It is likely that the broch was already abandoned as a permanent dwelling before this activity took place, although doubtless its roofless shell was used from time to time over the ensuing centuries.

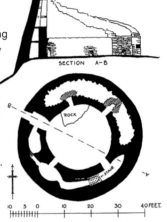

Plan in 1921 – note the vagueness where collapsed masonry obscured details.

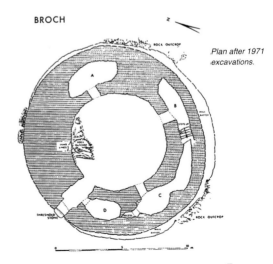

Plan after 1971 excavations.

A Carloway Legend : Morrisons against MacAulays

The most famous house of the broch in later years was by the Morrisons of Ness, who according to tradition sheltered there after being caught red-handed during a cattle raid on the lands of the local MacAulay clan. They retired inside and blocked the entrance, only to be smoked out by one Donald Cam MacAulay, who climbed the outer wall and threw down burning heather, forcing the Morrisons out to face their summary fate. This story, if it really dates to the 16th century as supposed, would imply that the walls were reasonably completed as late as that date.

Brochs and the Scottish Iron Age

Brochs and the Scottish Iron Age

Dun Carloway is one of the best preserved of all broch towers, but it may also have been one of the last to be built, perhaps sometime in the last century BC. The story of the brochs, however, began many centuries earlier.

Atlantic roundhouse/broch distribution in Scotland.

The 'invasion hypothesis'

Earlier generations of archaeologists thought that broch towers were built by invaders from southern England displaced by the Roman invasion of AD 43. Such 'invasionist' ideas were typical of the way in which archaeological remains used to be interpreted. It was thought that all great innovations in technology or culture could be traced to the Near East, or to the classical migration or trade, they eventually spread to the far corners of Europe.

Given this world view, it is easy to see why brochs were regarded for so long as the work of invaders or immigrants who stamped their authority on the cultural backwaters of the far north and west. How else could such masterpieces of drystone architecture have emerged so far from the supposed centres of the 'civilised' world?

It is true that there are some similarities between pottery and jewellery found in early broch excavations and first-century items from the south. But most of these objects were of fairly common currency in the British Iron Age and hardly amount to evidence of invasion. Most importantly, however, nothing even remotely resembling a broch tower, nor for that matter any drystone building of such architectural complexity, has ever been found in the areas from which these invaders supposedly came.

The birth of the brochs

Most recently, a series of important excavations in Orkney has shed new light on the origins of brochs. Around 600 BC, it seems that some communities there began building massive-walled, drystone roundhouses. Many archaeologist see these as the direct ancestors of the later broch tower. This does not mean, however, that brochs necessarily originated in Orkney: equally early versions may well await discovery elsewhere – in the Wester Isles, Shetland or Caithness.

These houses, like the excavated examples at Bu, lacked the complex internal features visible at Carloway and other broch towers, and they probably appeared from the outside as imposing, but haredly tower-like buildings. Many were isolated structures, perhaps the homes of prosperous farmers.

They were simply an Atlantic Scottish variant of the architectural fashion for roundhouse building favoured throughout much of the British Isles at the time.

Remains of the floor at the early broch-like structure at Bu, in Orkney.

A typical Iron Age roundhouse from lowland Britain.

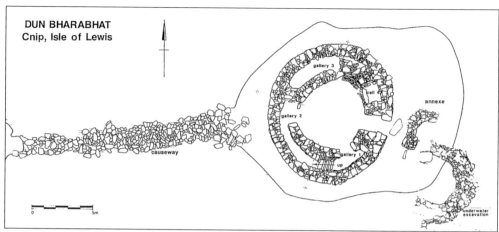

DUN BHARABHAT
Cnip, Isle of Lewis

gallery 3
cell
annexe
gallery 2
causeway
gallery 1
up
underwater
excavation

0   5m

Dun Bharabhat, Cnip – plan of site as excavated and artist's reconstruction.

Broch architecture

In the following centuries rather more complex round-houses developed, some with cells and galleries built within their thick stone walls. The walls of Dun Bharabhat in Lewis, for example, contained several cells and galleries, and a stair leading to a now-vanished first floor, or perhaps to the roof. Unlike the large timber round-houses of south-east Scotland, or of Wessex, which had more or less disappeared long before the end of the Iron Age, these Atlantic roundhouses continued to evolve until the start of the Christian era and culminated in massive broch towers like Mousa in Shetland and Dun Carloway itself.

In their fully developed form, brochs reached heights of more than 13m: for structures built without mortar this was an astonishing achievement. These would have been grim and imposing buildings with only a single, low, narrow entrance to puncture the stony outer shell.

The broch of Mousa in Shetland – the stonework survives almost complete, 13m tall.

The typical broch tower was formed of two concentric walls bounded together at intervals by banks of stone slabs to form a series of internal galleries and stairs. Ledges, or 'scarcements', projecting from the inner wall would have supported upper timber floors and the conical thatched roof. While the galleries and stairs would have let people to move between floors, they usually became too narrow in their upper parts to allow easy access to the wall-head.

Perhaps most intriguingly, the interior wall faces of many broch towers are interrupted by vertical arrangements of small openings. Mousa has four such 'voids'.

One theory is that this served to ease the weight of stone above the entrances to cells and galleries, yet this seems an unlikely justification for the creation of what weems to have been dangerous weak points in the structure.

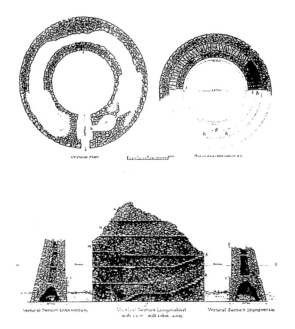

The cross section through Dun Carloway, showing the structure between the skins of stone walling.

Voids in the inner wall-face may have reduced stress or aided air circulation – these are at Mousa.

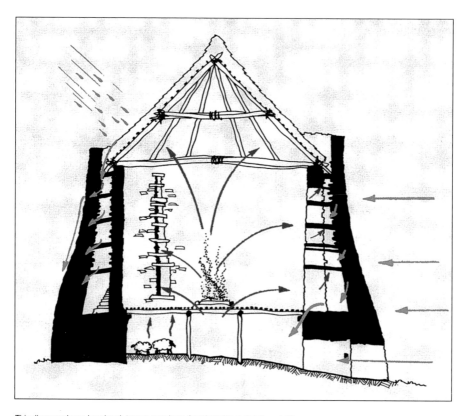

This diagram shows how broch towers may have functioned to maintain a stable, warm environment for their inhabitants. Based on an idea from John Hope.

Recent studies of broch architecture have begun to suggest exactly why broch towers took the for they did. The architect John Hope has suggested that they were carefully tailored to the cold and windy conditions of Atlantic Scotland. In winter, the galleries within the walls would have prevented wind-driven rain and snow from penetrating the central rooms, while the 'voids' would have let heat from the hearth circulate, keeping the galleries dry. In summer, the galleries would have let heat from the sun circulate around the building.

Often the ground floor interiors were poorly finished, with irregular walling and protruding rocky outcrops, while the hollow wall construction usually began only at first floor level. A combination of these factors suggests that the main area for human habitation was on the timber first floor. Heat from animas stalled below might have added to the warmth of the house.

Castle or farmhouse?

Alan Braby's reconstruction shows how the stone tower was equipped as a comfortable yet secure dwelling.

Castle or farmhouse?

Excavations over the years have shown that, although their tall, thick walls would doubtless have deterred casual intruders, brochs were essentially elaborate and defensible farmhouses rather than occasional refuges from pirates, slave raiders, or hostile neighbours. Structures like Dun Carloway could have housed an extended family, and probably some of their livestock, at least over the winter. The livestock would have provided an additional source of heat, as they did in later Hebridean blackhouses, and their manure would have been collected and spreads on the fields. However, in the tight confines of a broch the presence of animals would have meant much water-carrying, since most brochs had no wells.

Yet brochs were clearly not simple functional structures. Traditional house style in the Hebrides have always tended to sit low against the winds rather than rise tower-like on already exposed knolls or islets. They have also tended to have relatively small roofing spans to conserve scarce timber: brochs, by contrast, would have made heavy demands on the fragile woodlands of the islands for their great conical roofs and timber floors, perhaps necessitating importation of timber from the mainland.

Such wilful disregard for scarce resources, and the desire for display inherent in the building of towers suggest that, more than simply houses, brochs were ostentatious symbols of wealth and status.

Ideas have changed. The pent roof is not a solution archaeologists today would favour, but was popular in 1950s-1980s reconstruction drawing.

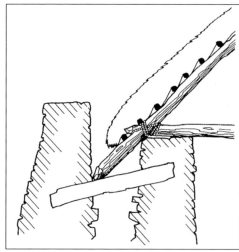

Ideas continue to change. Since the splendid drawing on page 15 was commissioned, the authors have come up with a new roofing detail which allows access to the wall-head for repair and lookout.

The 'broch villages' of Orkney and Caithness (such as this one at Gurness in Orkney) find no reflection in the Western Isles, where brochs seem to have been isolated farmsteads, with a few outbuildings at best. This presumably reflects major differences in society between the two regions in the Iron Age.

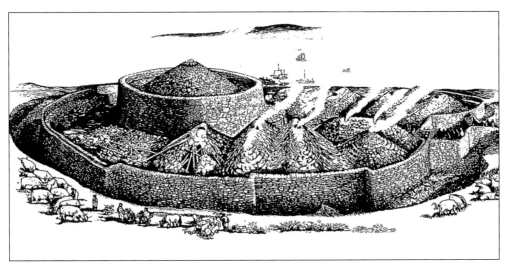

Gurness – Artist's impression showing the broch and its encircling cluster of houses.

Selection of Iron Age Pottery from sites in Lewis.

Personal jewellery, whetstones and crucibles for bronze working found at Iron Age sites in Lewis.

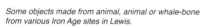

Some objects made from animal, animal or whale-bone from various Iron Age sites in Lewis.

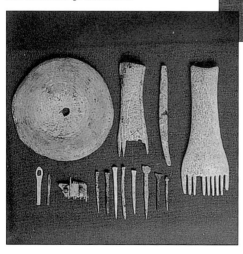

The broch dwellers of the Western Isles had a rich material culture. This is a selection of the decorated pottery styles typical of period.

Brochs and the land

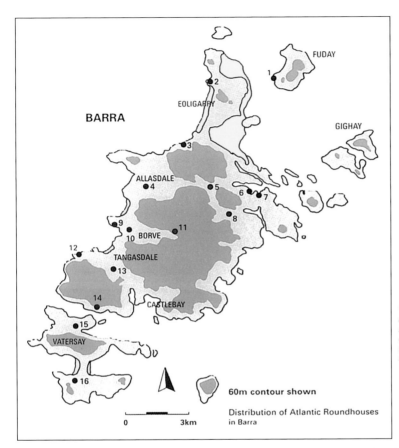

The brochs of Barra seem to occupy discrete landscape blocks that probably corresponded with the land held and farmed by the broch-dwelling family.

Distribution of Atlantic Roundhouses in Barra

60m contour shown

Although built to impress, the sheer numbers of brochs in the island show that they were not restricted to senior tribal chiefs or leaders. Indeed, in Barra and North Uist, where a lot of survey work has been carried out, there are approximately the same numbers of brochs as there were tenant farmers in the 18th century.

Perhaps not surprisingly, then Hebridean brochs vary considerably in size, complexity and location. While fine broch towers like Dun Carloway were probably built by local leaders, others, like the relatively small Dun Bharabhat in Lewis, probably served land-holding families of much lesser rank. In all cases, however, the broch symbolised the aspirations of its builders and occupants, stamping their authority on the landscape and supporting their pretensions to high social standing.

Dun Cuier in Barra typifies the landscape setting of brochs; set on the summit of a low hill it dominates the surrounding farmland.

Many Hebridean broch sites were occupied over many generations and rebuilt many times. In Loch an Duin, near Shader in Lewis, the remains of an earlier fortification can be seen just below water to the right of the broch and it may be that the pale patch to its upper left also lies over an earlier settlement.

Dun Carloway Today

Dun Carloway forms an impressive skyline, seen from the Visitor Centre.

Dun Carloway Today

The broch is prominent when approached from the south-east past roofless croft buildings (probably constructed with stones from the broach). The site's natural defensibility, combined with local prominence, would have been a magnet for the brooch-builders. The broch stands on a knoll on the steep hillside, its entrance facing north-west, away from the line of approach. The visitor, today as in the Iron Age, must walk around the curve of the wall to reach the door, gaining a clear impression of the bulk and strength of the structure.

The broch has partly collapsed, providing a cross-section. Its stone structure is complete only in the lowest level, with a jagged portion rising above. Like a cut-away drawing, this displays the hollow-wall structure to great effect.

Low lintels over the entrance passage force the modern visitor to stoop, just like visitors in the Iron Age. Part way down the passage are rebates in the stonework for the frame of al long-vanished wooden door. Beyond this, on the right, is a 'guard cell', a chamber which may have housed a gate-keeper. In some brochs, the door-bar slid back into this chamber. More prosaically, it may have housed a guard-dog or been a store for wet clothes and damp peats.

Once through the entrance passage, one can stand upright to look around. In the iron Age this might have been less easy, as wooden structures probably occupied the

Looking out. This passage was once lintelled over. Note the 'checks' in the stonework which once held the frame for a wooden doorway, secured by a stout wooden bar behind it.

interior. Typical features of broch architecture are obvious : apertures in the inner wallface at ground floor level, ladder,-like gaps in the upper welfare and the hollow-wall construction. More careful observation reveals a horizontal ledge above the lower apertures, and bedrock protruding from the floor. Just above the bedrock are vertical joins in the masonry which were once thought to show the entrance to another chamber, but these seem to be simply an old repair.

The three lower apertures lead into an oval chamber (on the left), a chamber with access to the stair (in the middle) and a passage running back under the stair (on the right). Throughout the middle aperture, a stairway with narrow steps leads some way up within the wall, but has been broken off by the partial collapse of the broch. The ladder-like voids in the upper wallface give light to the stair and reduce the weight of masonry over its entrance, and may have helped warm, dry air to circulate around the broch, as suggested on page 14.

The hollow walls are spanned by levels of lintel stones every 2 metres or so. These form 'galleries' in the wall, perhaps for storage. It used to be thought that these narrow corridors were living spaces, but archaeologists now think that they were primarily a constructional device, a sort of internal scaffolding which reduce the amount of stone needed and provided a builders' platform as the structure rose, and also allowed for later maintenance. Only at Mousa, in Shetland, are all the galleries wide enough to have been used as storage or living space. At all other tall brochs which survive, Dun Carloway included, the upper galleries are too narrow for access and have rough inner surfaces which certainly would not encourage domestic comfort.

Two meters up the inner wallface, the horizontal scarcement ledge probably supported the outer edge of a raised wooden floor. This was the main living area, with the ground floor relegated to storage or used to house animals. The protruding bedrock also suggests that the ground level

Looking up the internal stairway.

23

was not the main floor, or it would surely have been quarried away. Unfortunately for the archaeologist, all of the wooden structures which made the broch tower habitable have vanished, leaving only the stone shell.

Leaving the broch, turn left to example the foot of the broch tower, which is fitted ingeniously on the irregular outcrop.
Take care on the slipper grass; it is best to return to the broch entrance and leave by the north side.

Note how the stonework dovetails around the irregular bedrock.

Hollow wall

Voids

Scarcement

Entrance to cell

Caring for the broch

Early 20th century photograph showing the state of the broch before consolidation. Note the large gaps in the teetering stonework which have since been filled. More subtly, the lower part of the wall appears nowadays to have been raised by a level of large blocks and a turf capping. However, the careful dovetailing of the foundation onto the bedrock on the outside of the broch is not modern, but a genuine Iron Age feature.

In the centuries between the Iron Age and the present day the crumbling walls of the broch must have provided shelter on many occasions. Certainly they seem to have been reasonably intact until the 16th century. But by the mid 19th century the large portion of the upper wall had gone, and its stones had been carried away for building elsewhere. To stop further depreciations it became one of the very first legally protected 'scheduled' ancient monuments in Scotland, in 1882, and passed into State care five years later.

Since 1887, great efforts have been made to ensure that Dun Carloway does not deteriorate. If it is hard to see the evidence for this maintenance, this is a compliment to the skilled masons who replace cracked stones, re-insert pinning (the small stones between the large blocks) as frost dislodges them and sometimes rebuilt sections of the wall.

The principal threat today is the wind. The original structure presented a smooth, curved face to the wind, but now the open wall-ends catch the winter gales and vibrate, loosening stones. This has made it necessary to reinforce them over the years, with metal bars and tie-stones inserted to prevent further collapse.

Beyond the Brochs

The wheelhouse at Cnip under excavation.

Wheelhouses

We will never know precisely why people stopped building brochs. It is possible that the demands that they placed on timber for floors and roofing eventually became too great. Or perhaps the emergence of new leaders with power over much wider areas discouraged the self-aggrandisement of petty local land-holders.

Whatever the reasons, by the last century BC brochs seem to have been largely replaced, at least as the standard dwelling of the day, by a radically different house form. Wheelhouses were so-called because of their distinctive plan. They were often quite impressive buildings, requiring great skill in drystone building. But unlike brochs they were impressive only from inside, where the intricate stone piers (the 'spokes' of the 'wheel') rose to form a circle of arches around the hearth. From outside they were unprepossessing; little more than roofs projecting above the sand hills or ruined brochs into which they were generally built.

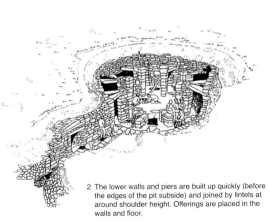

1 Building stone is stacked in a great pit dug into the coastal sand dune.

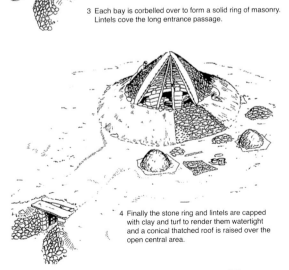

3 Each bay is corbelled over to form a solid ring of masonry. Lintels cove the long entrance passage.

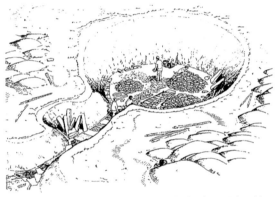

2 The lower walls and piers are built up quickly (before the edges of the pit subside) and joined by lintels at around shoulder height. Offerings are placed in the walls and floor.

4 Finally the stone ring and lintels are capped with clay and turf to render them watertight and a conical thatched roof is raised over the open central area.

27

The end of the brochs

Although brochs had probably ceased to be built by the end of the 1st century BC, many were still occupied. At Loch na Berie in Lewis, excavations by Edinburgh University have revealed a lengthy sequence of later houses built within the ruins of the tower. These show that the broch continued to be an important settlement until the Viking period, around AD 800.

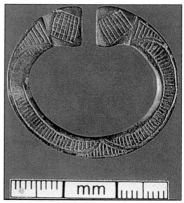

In the Pictish period jewellery and personal appearance seems to have been a more important indicator of status than the monumental houses of the Iron Age. This brooch from Loch na Berie dates to the middle of the 1st millennium AD and suggests links with both Ireland and Anglo-Saxon Northumbria.

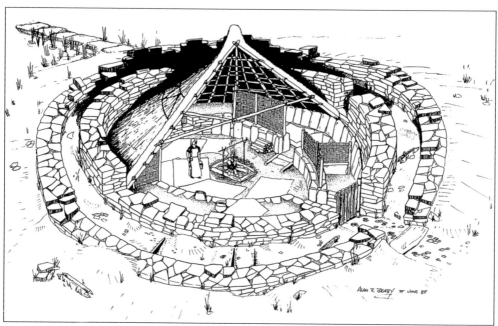

By around AD 500 the Western Isles were probably part of the Pictish kingdom. This cellular building, built in the ruins of the Loch na Berie broch, was probably the home of a powerful Pictish family.

These three views show the Pictish period settlement at Bosta. The cellular houses visible here are typical of the period between the decline of the brochs and the arrival of the Vikings.

Like its neighbouring monument, the Standing Stones of Calanais, the Broch has an aura and presence which holds a fascinating for all who visit it. The Doune Broch Centre, *Ionad an Dùin Mhòir,* is discreetly located nearby the Broch and is owned and managed by the local Trust, *Urras nan Tursachan,* which seeks to promote and strengthen pride in the deep past of the Outer Hebrides. Providing visitors with a much better understanding of the site's history is part of a wider effort to heighten public awareness of the complex heritage, both natural and built, of the west side of Lewis.

OTHER SITES TO VISIT

The Western Isles possess a large number of Iron Age brochs and duns, as well as other Iron Age sites. This is a select list of the best and most significant in terms of archaeological research, but, for anyone whose enthusiasm is whetted, the 1:50000 Ordnance Survey maps show many more locations. Remember that many of the loch island duns are not usually accessible, but can be viewed from the adjacent shore, and that most sites can only be visited by crossing croftland: if in any doubt, enquire locally. Several of these sites are on the routes of established walks, with useful leaflets available in local Tourist Information Offices.

These sites are arranged from north to south, and their OS grid references are given.

Lewis

Dùn Borve, Borve – broch   NB 418580

In an unusual position on a flat, bare, moorland, the lower part of the wall survives, but has been heavily robbed over the years. 400m NE from Mealabost road end.

Dùn Loch an Dùin, Shader – broch   NB 393542

Traces of wall structure and a fine causeway, with the 'ghost' of an earlier similar structure in the water just to the south, appearing just slightly above the loch.
Along loch shore from road which leads to Steinacleit.

Dùn Bharabhat, Great Bernera – broch   NB 156355

A small broch or large dun, set on a tiny island and accessed by a perilous causeway. Leave Barraglom to Breaclete road 500m N of Kirkibost junction, then 800m over moorland to S of Loch na Ceannamboir to reach E shore of Loch Bharabhat.

Bosta ,Great Bernera – houses   NB 136403

Excavation in 1996 following coastal erosion revealed several houses set into sand. The plan of these is laid out for visitors, and it is hoped to build a replica nearby.
Park at Bosta road end (signposted 'to the shore'), then follow signs past cemetery.

Dùn Bharabhat, Cnip – dùn   NB 102352

Dun on loch island with fine causeway: the causeway was ruinous until 'repaired' to provide access for archaeological excavation in 1986.
From caravan site near shore, 700m to SW following small stream: note ruins of small mills.

Loch na Berie, Cnip – broch and later structures   NB 099353

Currently undergoing seasonal excavation, this broch has been partly submerged by changes in water level. Access tends to be damp and does not follow the ancient causeway.
Park near bend of road just W of Berie, and follow the fenced path to S.

North Uist

Dùn an Sticer – broch   NB 897777

Another fine loch island broch with causeway. Park beside road 2km S from Berneray/Harris ferry landing (and terminal for proposed causeway to Berneray), then short walk over open grassland.

Dùn Thorcuill – broch   NB 888737

In an area of rather barren moorland, it is hard to see why Iron Age inhabitants valued this area enough to build this typical loch island fortification.
Park 300m along Lochportain road and then walk 500m N around SW shore of loch.

South Clettraval – wheelhouse seto into burial ground
NF 749713

This structure, now ruinous, is a wheelhouse set into the forecourt of a Neolithic chambered burial tomb. Later in its life the wheelhouse was modified and then replaced by a much slighter building. A sub-rectangular building nearby may have been a cattle-byre, while to the W is a stretch of walling that may once have marked the edge of a farmyard around the house. Most Iron Age houses so far found have been near the shore, but there are few, like South Clettraveal, on upland sites.
Take the South Clettraval road opposite Tigharry junction, parking (carefully) near cattlegrid just S of hilltop.

South Uist

Dùn Vulan, – dun/broch   NF 713297

Recently excavated, this site is of particular
interest for its location (2000 years ago the
shore lay to the W, and the broch stood on a
loch island) and for extensive evidence
for later buildings found under the storm
beach to the S.

Following Bornish road almost to the end of
Rubha Ardvule. (The recent structures nearby
are the remains of missile testing facilities
from the 1950s and 1960s).

Kilphedir – wheelhouse   NF 733203

Now rather ruinous, this wheelhouse
occupies a typical location set in sand. It was
excavated in the 1950s.

Take shore road NW from Kilphedir, parking
where the road curves to the SW. The
wheelhouse is in the grassed-over sand hill
to the NW.

Barra and The Southern Isles

Dùn Cuier – broch   NF 664034

A hilltop broch which was re-utilised later as
a roundhouse.

Park near the cemetery and climb SE up a
steep grassy hill: take care crossing fences.

Allasdale – wheelhouse   NF 677022

Grassed-over remains of a wheelhouse set at
head of a valley, in what have
been rich grazing land. The site layout is
obscured by later shieling huts, used during
summer grazing.

Take minor road to Craigston, parking as for
thatched cottages, then climb NE past the
massive Dùn Bharpa (a Neolithic chambered
burial tomb, despite the 'dùn name) to drop
down into head of the Allasddae valley.

Dùn a' Chaolais, Vatersay – broch and fields   NL 628970

A ruined broch with stone walls radiating out
from it, emphasising the point that broch-
dwellers were farmers, this is one of the few
good examples of an Iron Age field system in
the Western Isles.

Park beside road from causeway as it crosses
shoulder of Ben Oronsay, then 200m to W.

Sandray – dùn   NL 637914

This small hilltop dun has one of the finest
settings of any Iron Age site, on a high
shoulder on the steep side of Cairn Galtar.
Sandray is uninhabited, but can usually be
visited subject to availability of a suitable
boat. Contact Castlebay Tourist Office for
details of local boat hire (01871 810336).

FURTHER READING

• Armit, I 1990 *Beyond the Brochs*

• Armit, I 1996 *The Archaeology of Skye and the Western Isles*

• Armit, I 1997 *Celtic Scotland*

• Fojut, J; Pringle, D and Walker, B 1994 *The Ancient Monuments of the Western Isles*

• Ritchie, J N G and Harman, M 1997 *Exploring Scotland's Heritage: Argyll and the Western Isles*